ANIMAL DANGER ZONE

GILA MONSTER!

Willow Clark

WINDMILL
BOOKS

New York

Published in 2011 by Windmill Books, LLC
303 Park Avenue South, Suite # 1280, New York, NY 10010-3657

CREDITS:
Author: Willow Clark
Edited by: Jennifer Way
Designed by: Brian Garvey

Photo Credits: Cover, pp. 4, 6, 7 (top, bottom), 9, 11 (top, bottom), 13 (bottom), 16 (bottom), 21 (top, bottom), 22 (bottom) Shutterstock.com; p. 5 © www.iStockphoto.com/Christine Glade; pp. 8, 22 (top) Mary Ann McDonald/Getty Images; p. 10 © Wayne Lynch/age fotostock; pp. 12, 14, 18 Jim Merli/Getty Images; p. 13 (top) © www.iStockphoto.com/kevdog818; p. 15 © www.iStockphoto.com/Bob Kupbens; p. 16 (top) © www.iStockphoto.com/Frank Leung; pp. 16-17 © Heuclin Daniel/age fotostock; p. 19 © C. Allan Morgan/Peter Arnold Inc.; p. 20 © www.iStockphoto.com/Windzepher.

Library of Congress Cataloging-in-Publication Data

Clark, Willow.
 Gila monster! / by Willow Clark.
     p. cm. — (Animal danger zone)
 Includes index.
 ISBN 978-1-60754-960-4 (library binding) — ISBN 978-1-60754-966-6 (pbk.) — ISBN 978-1-60754-967-3 (6-pack)
 1. Gila monster—Juvenile literature. I. Title.
 QL666.L247.C53 2010
 597.95'952—dc22

                                2010004428

Manufactured in the United States of America

For more great fiction and nonfiction, go to windmillbooks.com.

CPSIA Compliance Information: Batch #S10W: For further information contact Windmill Books, New York, New York at 1-866-478-0556.

TABLE OF CONTENTS

A Shy Monster

The Gila monster (pronounced HEE-luh MON-ster) is a **reptile** that lives in the southwestern United States and in northern Mexico. It is one of the world's few **venomous** lizards.

The Gila Monster lives in hot, dry desert areas like the one shown here.

4

The Gila monster might seem like a "monster" to the small animals it eats, but it doesn't often attack people.

Although the Gila monster has a scary name, it does not go out of its way to attack people. It spends most of its time in its **burrow**. It moves slowly, and only gives its painful bite when it thinks it is in danger.

The Gila monster is named for the Gila River. It was first found near this river, which runs through Arizona and New Mexico. This area is a desert **habitat**. Deserts are warm, dry, and sunny year-round.

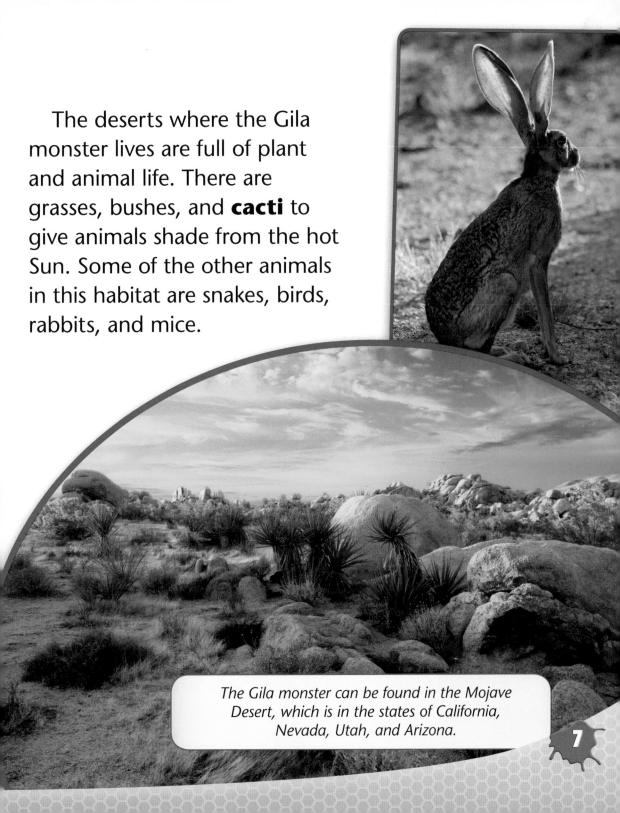

The deserts where the Gila monster lives are full of plant and animal life. There are grasses, bushes, and **cacti** to give animals shade from the hot Sun. Some of the other animals in this habitat are snakes, birds, rabbits, and mice.

The Gila monster can be found in the Mojave Desert, which is in the states of California, Nevada, Utah, and Arizona.

The Gila monster's tongue is divided into two points. This is called a "forked" tongue.

The Gila monster is North America's largest lizard. An adult is about 2 feet (.6 m) long and weighs about 5 pounds (2.3 kg). It has a fat tail, a forked tongue, and sharp claws on its feet.

The Gila monster's skin is covered in bumpy, bead-like scales.

The Gila monster's skin is black with bands of either yellow, pink, or orange. The scales are rounded and look like beads. This is why the Gila monster is known as a "beaded lizard."

Gila monsters spend most of their time in their burrow. They come out only to hunt for food or to sit in the sun. Like all reptiles, Gila monsters are **cold-blooded**. Sitting in the sun warms them up.

Gila monsters use their sharp claws to dig the underground burrows in which they live.

Between November and February, Gila monsters **hibernate**. Although desert winters are not as cold as winter in other places, it's cold enough to slow down cold-blooded animals' bodies. Hibernation lets the animal rest until the weather warms up again.

There are some plants that grow only in deserts, like the saguaro cactus shown here.

In Its Burrow

Gila monsters don't spend much of their time aboveground. When they do come out, they will feed upon many things. They eat eggs taken from bird nests, baby rabbits, and squirrels. A Gila monster can find an egg that is buried more than 6 inches (15 cm) under the ground.

In a zoo, Gila monsters eat two mice about two times per month.

Gila monsters eat baby rabbits.

The Gila monster can store fat in its oversized tail. It is able to go months between meals.

A Gila monster uses its tongue to pick up smells that can lead it to food, like these eggs.

Gila monsters do not have very good eyesight. When they hunt, they use their senses of taste and smell. To track **prey**, the Gila monster uses its forked tongue to pick up scents in the air.

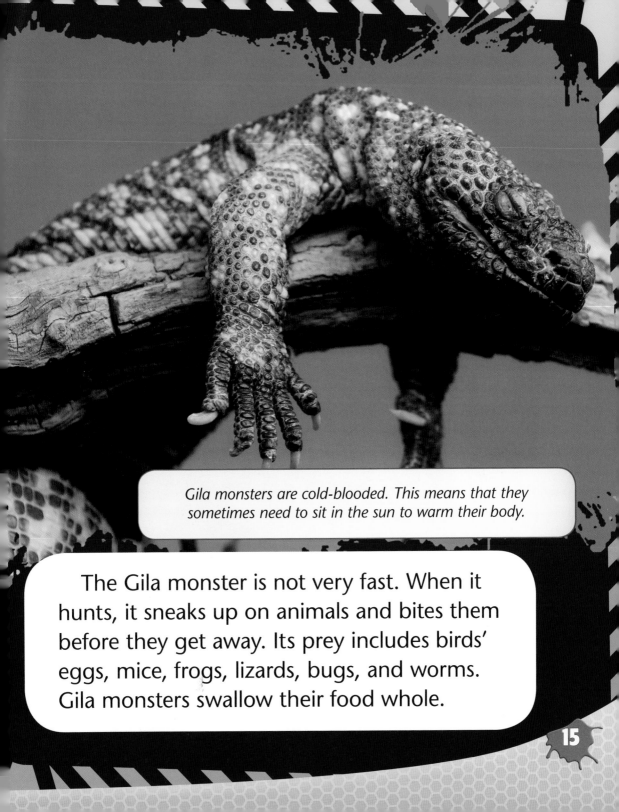

Gila monsters are cold-blooded. This means that they sometimes need to sit in the sun to warm their body.

The Gila monster is not very fast. When it hunts, it sneaks up on animals and bites them before they get away. Its prey includes birds' eggs, mice, frogs, lizards, bugs, and worms. Gila monsters swallow their food whole.

The Gila monster's powerful lower jaw holds its prey. It injects its venom through its grooved teeth. This venom stuns small prey such as birds, lizards, frogs, and insects.

When a Gila monster bites, the venom flows through the bite into the victim. The bite is very painful, but no people have died from the venom. The Gila monster only attacks people when it is bothered.

Gila Monster Eggs

When they are adults, Gila monsters **mate** from April to June. Female Gila monsters lay 2 to 12 eggs at a time. They bury the eggs underground. The eggs hatch after ten months.

The female digs a hole and lays eggs in the hole, and covers them. The eggs are not buried very deep, so the heat of the sun keeps them warm.

About ten months after the eggs are laid, baby Gila monsters break out of their eggs and crawl to the surface.

Baby Gila monsters are called hatchlings. Hatchlings are about 6 inches (15 cm) long and look like small Gila monsters. Gila monsters live for about 20 or more years in zoos. In the wild, they may live for even longer.

A Gila monster bite is rarely deadly to people. It may cause pain, swelling, bleeding, and sickness.

Above is a Gila monster skeleton. You can see the sharp, grooved teeth it uses to bite its prey.

In some parts of the American Southwest, people's homes are built near the Gila monster's natural habitat.

The biggest problem you might have if a Gila monster bites you is trying to get the lizard to let go of you!

But you really shouldn't worry. Gila monsters would rather run away from people and other large animals. To warn off possible predators, they will open their mouth very wide and hiss.

Did You Know?

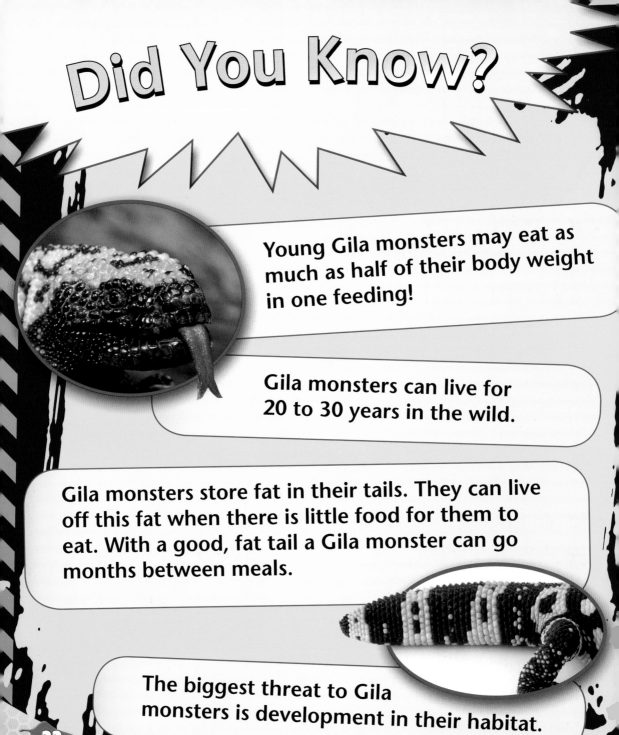

Young Gila monsters may eat as much as half of their body weight in one feeding!

Gila monsters can live for 20 to 30 years in the wild.

Gila monsters store fat in their tails. They can live off this fat when there is little food for them to eat. With a good, fat tail a Gila monster can go months between meals.

The biggest threat to Gila monsters is development in their habitat.

GLOSSARY

burrow (BUR-oh) A hole an animal digs in the ground for shelter.

cacti (KAK-ty) Plants that grow in dry, desert areas and have sharp spines instead of leaves.

cold-blooded (KOHLD-bluh-did) Having body heat that changes with the heat around the body.

habitat (HA-beh-tat) The kind of land where an animal or a plant naturally lives.

hibernate (HY-bur-nayt) To spend the winter in a sleeplike state.

mate (MAYT) To come together to make babies.

prey (PRAY) An animal that is hunted by another animal for food.

reptile (REP-tyl) A cold-blooded animal with thin, dry pieces of skin called scales.

venomous (VEH-nuh-mis) Having matter that can cause pain or death.

Index

Read More

Glaser, Jason. *Gila Monsters*. Mankato, MN: Capstone Press, 2006.

Lockwood, Sophie. *Gila Monsters*. Mankato, MN: Child's World, 2006.

Storad, Conrad. *Gila Monsters*. Minneapolis, MN: Lerner Publications, 2007.

Web Sites

For Web resources related to the subject of this book, go to: www.windmillbooks.com/weblinks and select this book's title.